# Tantra Massage:

## Sensual Massage Guide to Tantra Massage with Illustrated Tantra Techniques

ROZELLA HART

# Bonus: Book Club Invite

Before we get started with this Tantra Massage book, we wanted to tell you how much we appreciate you as a reader, and that we want to invite you to our Free Book Club.

When you subscribe, you get first access to discounted and free new releases from or small publishing house, Walnut Publishing.

Claim your invite at www.walnutpub.com.

Thanks for buying, and enjoy reading.

# NOTE FROM THE AUTHOR

Thank you for purchasing "Tantra Massage: Sensual Massage Guide to Tantra Massage with Illustrated Tantra Techniques."

I hope you will learn a lot of valuable information that you can apply to your own life, as well as have some fun and be entertained!

I worked hard to write this book with you, my reader, in mind. Whether you enjoyed the book, or you think I got some things wrong, I'd love to hear from you.

I personally read all my reviews on Amazon, and love to hear from my readers. If you can take a minute to just write at least one line about what you thought of my book, I'd be really grateful.

Type this URL into your browser to go straight to the review page for this book: bitly.com/tantricreview

I really appreciate it, and now, let's get to the book!

—Rozella Hart

# TABLE OF CONTENTS

# 1 Introduction

Congratulations on downloading Tantra Massage: A How-To Instructional Guide! If you have downloaded this book, then you are curious about all things involving tantric massages. Whether you are curious to know what they are or what they entail, this book will guide you through the history of tantra before talking you through how you and your partner can experience all the spiritual releases the tantric massage has to offer.

This book features unique techniques, hand motions, and positions through which a tantric massage can be utilized, and it will talk you through the various mental states and physical ailments that can benefit from a tantric massage. And, if you are still struggling to figure out whether a tantric massage is right for you, then we will outline exactly who will benefit from one and exactly how they will benefit from it!

This book is not just a boring history book, nor is it a book that just has erotic pictures. The illustrations in this guide provide so much more to you than "new positions." If you think a tantric massage is an erotic act meant to chase simple and brief moments of pleasure, then it is time to learn how much more tantra can be. We will address myths created by western cultures that have permeated through the idea of tantric, we will dispel those myths by giving you the accurate information you seek, and we will outline for you exactly where these myths developed and our theories as to why they did. The idea of a tantric massage being nothing but a pleasure-seeking device used during sex is the Western world's distortion of what a tantric massage really is.

And we are here to clear up any misunderstandings you might have.

There are many things this book promises, like eye-opening experiences and accurate education on the subject of tantric massages... but what I can personally promise is that, by the end of this book, you will fully know and understand what a tantric massage's purpose truly is, why it was designed in the first place, where it originates from, and whether a tantric massage is right for you. And, as if all of that wasn't enough, this book will give you specific techniques you can use in order to begin your journey towards the healing spiritual power the tantric massage has to offer if performed right.

And trust me, we will walk you through exactly how to give, and receive, a tantric massage.

If you have been curious about the subject, then do not delay any longer. Purchase this book if you have not done so already and dive in to discover the truth that will set you and your partner free in the bedroom. The entire purpose of spiritual connection has been tossed out in favor of chasing something much quicker and more temporary in some guides, but not this one. We will get to the real core of spirituality, pleasure and eroticism. Do not delay your purchase! If you have already taken the plunge, I thank you very much for putting your trust in me. If you have not, I urge you to go ahead and take the chance. Do not allow yourself to be fed anymore lies when it comes to something as pure, something as healing, and something as beautiful as a tantric massage.

Welcome to the misunderstood world of the tantric massage. Cast aside everything you think you know, open your mind to the spiritual world that surrounds your physical self, and dive headfirst into a world not solely to give you sexual release, but to give you spiritual satisfaction as well, and pleasure and feelings you never thought possible before.

## 2  HISTORY OF TANTRIC MASSAGE

THE TANTRA BELIEF ORIGINATED IN what we now know as India at least 5000 years ago. The belief predates both Hinduism and Buddhism, and, in many ways, influences both religions. However, there is one big difference between Tantra and any religion it influences: Physical fulfillment and spiritual growth are not mutually exclusive. Many religions focus on either one or the other to bloom in a person's life, but Tantra focuses on both of them as ideal in order to obtain a well-rounded life. The core belief of Tantra is that without one of these sides of the coin, you cannot have the other.

Tantrics, or those who believe in the teachings of Tantra, understand that working on their bodies can clear toxins and other negative effects from the system, which can in turn enable physical healing, as well as a re-integration with the body's spirit and the spiritual energy that surrounds us on a daily basis. The belief in the energy force the universe brings us is a central belief of Tantra, and it preaches that the life force that swells within our bodies is the same energy pulsating through the universe. Along this same thinking, however, is the understanding that the repression or neglect of this energy leaves the physical body damaged and feeling unbalanced, which results in emotional, mental, and physical issues and/or ailments one might not understand how to correct.

The belief in Tantra completely rejects the idea of repressing physical fulfillment in any form because this belief understands that fulfilling the basic biological urges of our bodies keeps us in open communication with the universe's energies. When the body pays attention to its needs, there is happiness and fulfillment which can bring about a positive spiritual life force, but when physical fulfillment is denied, there are pains and damages inflicted that are unnecessary.

If you would not starve your body of food or water, which are both base biological urges, why would you deny your body physical fulfillment? Many would argue that denying this basic instinct would lead to less disease and fewer unwanted pregnancies, and yes, this may be true.

But let me present this argument: if you do not sanitize your water, what happens? Not pregnancy, of course, but diseases and flesh-eating bacteria work their way into your body. Does this mean you simply don't drink water? No! You make sure that your water has been filtered and disinfected!

What about food? You wouldn't consume raw meat, right? It would make you sick. It could infect you with salmonella, E. coli, or another illness that could put you in the hospital. These dangers don't mean that you don't eat meat, they mean that you simply cook your food to safe levels to consume.

So, why is physical fulfillment denied because of consequences that can be prevented by taking precautions?

The first issue is the idea that tantric massage is erotic. If something is erotic, its sole purpose is to bring sexual pleasure. That is not the point of a tantric massage. A tantric massage is born out the Tantra belief, which beckons individuals to open their minds and their bodies to the energies around them that the universe wants them to experience.

And no, that is not a fancy way of saying "orgasm."

The belief in Tantra rejects the idea of physical repression. When little attention is paid to the body's needs, terrible things result: insufficient water results in dehydration, insufficient food results in the shutting down of organs, and insufficient physical fulfillment results in a disconnect with the universe around us that can then lead to unresolved anger issues, abandonment issues, and self-esteem issues.

All of which can become crippling to someone's everyday life.

Tantrics believe that growing as a complete human being means not only fulfilling the basic biological urges of the body, but also ridding the body of blockages that have built up over time because of repressive states. Most major religions believe we are more than just our physical body, so relieving psychic as well as physical blockages is imperative to realigning our souls with the universe around us. This powerful spirit energy we are repressing and should be tapping into, according to Tantrics, is situated between our legs. Why? Because that is where all life comes from (with regard to humans). That is where a person's connection with the universe begins: between the legs of another.

This energy then rises up through our system and courses through our veins, and if this energy remains repressed or dormant, it means our knowledge and emotional intelligence is limited. But, if it is awakened and released (again, not a fancy euphemism for "orgasm"), spiritual growth is not only obtained, but catalyzed.

# 3  How is Tantric Massage Different?

So, what separates a tantric massage from other types of massages, such as a hot stone massage or a Swedish massage? For one, therapeutic massages only focus on direct physical benefits. Those who seek a tantric massage are out to align their souls and energies with the universe around them, which requires movements of the hands and the touching of the Base Chakra, which is the area of the body that houses the root of our spiritual energies.

Tantrics believe that pleasure derived from a tantric massage is the gateway to obtaining one's own level of spirituality and one's own relationship with the spiritual energies that surround our bodies. While a tantric massage offers many physical benefits that we will discuss later, the main goal of a tantric massage is to bind your inner energies to the surrounding universal energies.

A tantric massage is also given without seeking any sort of compensation. Many people who perform physical massages expect some sort of payment or praise, but those who administer tantric massages seek no other incentive but to help their partner. It is a selfless act that requires nothing in return. It is not an attempt to simply stimulate an orgasm from another individual or to make oneself proud: it is just to aid the other's spiritually-binding process.

Another difference between tantric massages and regular massages is the fact that no barriers are imposed when giving one. In a regular massage, towels and undergarments are used as barriers between the giver of the massage and the one receiving it. In a tantric massage, none of these barriers exist. It is a complete connection between two people, and when consent is given, can result in exploration beyond achieving a simple orgasm.

Tantric massages also come with specific breathing techniques to be performed while the massage is taking place. A regular massage does not have these types of relaxation techniques that the person being massaged is required to perform. This type of personal relaxation while the individual is being massaged results in inward stress relief as well as outward stress relief.

The belief in Tantra is a belief in letting go of societally-imposed ideologies and gaining a type of freedom that many do not have. It is about aligning the body with the universal energies around us as well as experiencing and experimenting with ways your own body opens itself up to the heavens. It can be liberating when you boil your body down to its base urges and find that, by fulfilling these urges, you balance yourself out and become a more stable individual and human being.

This is what Tantra preaches, and this is why the tantric massage is more than an erotic experience.

# 4 BENEFITS OF TANTRIC MASSAGE

THERE ARE TWO MAIN BENEFITS you receive when you receive a tantric massage: physical and emotional intimacy. There is an innate foundation of trust that must occur between two people before tantric massages can be explored, and that enhances the emotional intimacy further. When your body is relaxed and thriving, it is open to the cosmic energies that surround it. This physical closeness with your partner who is administering the massage enables you to feel safe, thereby opening up your psychic stores to the energies the universe wishes you to receive. Not only that, but the emotional intelligence that comes from accepting freely what the universe has to give aids the individual receiving the massage in furthering their emotional journey.

If you are the person giving the massage, these two main benefits still exist. You get to learn your partner's body more intimately as well as learn what unlocks the deepest recesses of their mind. When you watch your partner's body relax before you, you learn how their body works in its most intimate of ways. This closeness further breeds the idea of trust and allows you to view and read your partner in ways you could have never imagined. Not only that, but you get to further your emotional capacity for your partner because their ability to hand over the catalyst of their universal connection to you means they trust you. This innate showing of trust can fuel deep emotional connections within your soul, and it can help you to learn how to foster that same trusting connection with your partner when it comes time for you to receive the massage.

Although those are considered the two main benefits, there are other benefits that come with receiving a tantric massage. One of the main reasons people seek out tantric massages is to help overcome a particular trauma in their lives. Whether that trauma was sexual or psychological, many childhood and adulthood traumas can result in people closing themselves off physically and emotionally to others. Tantric massages can be a way to reopening the mind, body, and spirit to receiving and fulfilling these two aspects of living that are required for a truly balanced well-being. In all tantric massage sessions, the recipient is in complete control. However, in sessions that are addressing particular traumas, there is usually a bit more talking involved. The masseuse usually talks the recipient through all the things they are doing and what they will do, and the masseuse pays great attention to how the recipient's body is reacting.

This not only keeps the recipient safe, but allows them to prepare themselves for what is coming up. If they hear something they are not willing to participate in, they can verbalize that by saying "pass" or "no," and that opens up a dialogue as to why. In this way, a tantric massage is not merely a way to cope physically with a trauma, it is a way to properly communicate the verbal aspect of that trauma. In many ways, the masseuse then turns into a sort of makeshift psychologist, providing an avenue for the recipient of the massage to converse freely and openly without judgment, pretense, or labels.

# 5  EASING STRESS WITH TANTRIC MASSAGE

A TANTRIC MASSAGE ALSO HELPS with general relaxation. If you have a high-stress career and have tension issues anywhere in your body, a tantric massage can help regularly alleviate that tension and stress. This can open up the body to its natural healing practices, which decreases the damage caused by the stress hormone cortisol.

One of the main things that separates tantric massages from regular massages are the breathing techniques. Whether your partner is talking you through them or a masseuse is, these breathing techniques not only further relaxation, but they help to cleanse and rid the body of toxins. These breathing techniques can help those experiencing flashbacks of trauma and individuals struggling to relax to calm their minds and souls, which just adds to the overall experience. Some masseuses or partners add aromatherapy into the mix, and depending on the mixture, deep breathing will help the recipient of the massage experience everything from a calming sleep to an opening of the mind.

These breathing techniques have another facet: the curbing of impulses. As fallible humans, when we suppress a natural part of our being (such as the intake of food, water, or physical closeness) we have a tendency to make rash and quick decisions. The breathing exercises allow us to take in the physical closeness we are experiencing, and because this is the most-deprived part of the body, the impulses someone might have come into the session with are suddenly curbed. Many men have preached that receiving a tantric massage helped them with their premature ejaculation issues and many women have reported that it relieved them of some of the emotional symptoms that usually occur before their menstrual cycles.

There is also a suggestion that tantric massage promotes self-awareness. When your chakras and energies are aligning with the universe around you, you can unlock truths about yourself you didn't understand before. Once you cast aside the job requirements, the stressors of work, or even the hardships in your relationships with family and/or friends, your body and your emotional state will pull from your subconscious truths you have been shoving down for quite some time. This self-awareness is not just healthy for the overall well-being, but it can come in handy when trying to make big decisions in your life. Many life-changing visions and emotions take place during tantric massages, for both the recipient and the giver.

Tantric massages also address basic physical well-being. The deep tissue, all-encompassing massage improves blood circulation in a way a regular massage does not. The decrease in your stress levels coupled with this increased blood circulation helps your body to further remove cortisol and toxins from your muscle and bones, and this aids your body's ability to heal. When people come out of a tantric massage rejuvenated and refilled on their energy stores, this is what has taken place: your body has been jump-started to heal itself and the energy stores you have unlocked are a result of those excess toxins being alleviated.

Tantric massages hold many benefits, all of which the recipient and the giver of the massage can partake in. It is a phenomenal tool in the kit of both professional masseuses and intimate couples that helps to promote bodily health, mental health, and emotional health. It doesn't just prompt a connection with the universe, it prompts a connection between two different people as well as an inward connection with one's true self.

Although we have made it clear that tantric massages are different from regular massages, we have also covered that tantric massages are not simply sexual acts. However, the greatest difference people see between tantric massages and regular massages is the fact that tantric massages can, and usually do (unless otherwise specified), infuse touches in erogenous zones in order to promote blood flow, relaxation, and intimacy. The term erogenous zone is most understood in reference to sexual situations, so we will cover its definition and its use in tantric massage in the next chapter.

# 6 WHAT IS AN EROGENOUS ZONE?

AN EROGENOUS ZONE IS A particular area of the body that has a heightened sensitivity to any sort of stimulation. Whether or not it generates a sexual response is null and void, the whole point of an erogenous zone is the fact that it is sensitive to stimulation. For example, scar tissue is not erogenous because it takes a great deal to stimulate it. However, the skin of the neck can be erogenous because it is sensitive to even the mere idea of touch. What makes this type of sensitive zone erogenous is its role within human sexuality and whether it can elicit the type of response someone wants it to when it comes to sexual foreplay or intercourse.

However, for the purposes of a tantric massage, an erogenous zone is any part of the body that is sensitive to the massaging touches of the masseuse.

The responses that can be generated via these touches are not always sexual: if the response to the massage movement is relaxation, then that is considered an erogenous zone. If the response to the massage is the prickling of the skin, then it is an erogenous zone. It does not have to lead to sexual arousal or orgasm in order to be considered erogenous, despite how the Western world has change the definition over time.

These zones are located all over the human body, but their sensitivity varies from zone to zone and person to person. It all depends on the concentration of nerve endings in that particular area. For example, the bottom of someone's feet might have more nerve endings than their earlobe, which is why their feet can be ticklish while their earlobe is not. However, the earlobe can become ticklish or sensitive with the right type of stimulation, such as light touches or the pulsating of breath. Then the earlobe becomes sensitive, and that sensitivity is what makes it erogenous.

The touching of someone's erogenous zones is an act of intimacy, which is what a tantric massage wants to encourage. This closeness between two individuals blooms when someone stimulates an erogenous zone on another person's body and receives a positive result, like a sigh or a giggle. It's why people enjoy tickling others, and it is why partners love giving their significant others massages that make them groan, murmur or moan: That positive feedback ensures they are doing something pleasurable and not doing something that hurts.

Erogenous zones, however, do have specific classifications depending on the type of response they stimulate when stimulated in a sexual environment. Many people can become gently aroused with caresses to their eyelids, temples, shoulders, and hands, while others can become greatly aroused when areas such as their buttocks, lower back, and neck are caressed. All of these areas (and more!) are targeted during tantric massages, and all serve to slowly relax the body and open it up to the sensual pleasures of the world around it.

Do not misconstrue this pleasure-seeking practice with seeking orgasm. That is not the purpose with a tantric massage, as we have mentioned before, but it is important to reiterate it. While some people use tantric massage as a vehicle to get to an orgasm, that should never be the "goal" of a tantric massage.

# 7 WHERE ARE THE EROGENOUS ZONES?

UNDERSTANDING WHERE THESE EROGENOUS ZONES lie and how the can be stimulated will help guide the beginner through the basics of a tantric massage. Hitting these spots and paying attention to them will allow the body its fill of physical pleasures without seeking something potentially harmful, and it will begin an individual's journey through opening their own body to the energies around them and receiving them without feeling guilty or scorned in the process.

In general, the erogenous zones on a female body are as such: the clitoris, the vagina, the cervix, the mouth and lips, the neck, the nipples, and the ears. When we hear most of these areas, the only thing that springs to mind is sexual release and arousal. However, with a tantric massage, these areas serve as the most sensitive areas to massage in order to not only improve blood circulation, but to relax and center the mind on the particular task at hand. Part of aligning the chakras with the universe is to clear all cluttering thoughts from the mind, and if someone is struggling to do that, the partner (or masseur) can begin to slowly massage these areas to help get them to focus.

The clitoris houses the most nerve endings in any one given area of the female body, and it is the runaway winner for those who wish to achieve orgasm. However, a tantric massage is not really about chasing an orgasm, so what is its role in tantric massage? The biggest role it plays is helping trauma victims take back their sexuality while slowly approaching their anxieties. When tantric massages are used for immersive therapy techniques, it will usually take the client a while to build up to allowing the masseuse to massage this area. If sexual trauma in any way has blocked their ability to receive this type of stimulation, sometimes it can take dozens of appointments before the anxiety is finally alleviated.

*The female erogenous zone, as highlighted in this illustration, are the clitoris, vagina cervix, mouth and lips, neck, nipples and ears.*

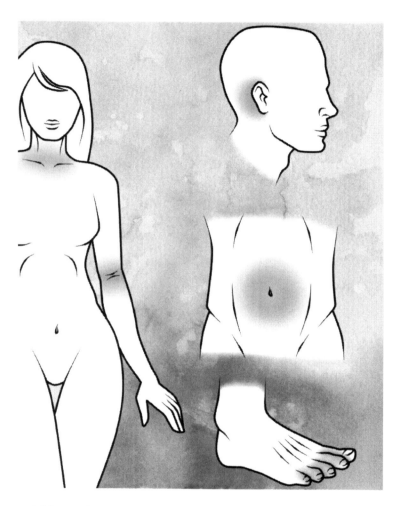

*Additional erogenous zones that may not be obvious are the neck, elbow, toes, stomach, and behind the ears.*

However, the clitoris (in this case) is what the masseuse is working towards. Once the masseuse can aid the patient in becoming comfortable with the touching of this organ, that is when both the recipient and the masseuse know the therapy has reached its culmination.

However, the clitoris might be bypassed in a tantric massage if the recipient is not comfortable with it or if their spiritual energies are aligning without its stimulation.

For those of you wondering how in the world a cervix is going to be stimulated in a tantric massage, fear not. This is not an actual body part that is stimulated during the massage because of its location within the body. Remember, a tantric massage is not sex nor is it about chasing any sort of orgasm. Same goes for the vagina. However, the labia is usually massaged in tantric massages because the blood flow and circulation in the area is considered the foundation for the Base Chakra and is especially important when it comes to aligning the body with the universal energies pulsating against it.

There are other areas of the body that can become erogenous, however, that we do not automatically associate with sexual arousal and foreplay. For example, if someone is becoming relaxed and allowing their body to release itself to the tide of the universe, places like the crook of the elbow and the base of the neck start to become sensitive. When these places that do not have many individual nerve endings become sensitive and open to the reception of touch, that is when the body is truly beginning to relax and align itself with the world surrounding it. This is the ultimate goal of a tantric massage: to circulate the blood in every single outer part of the body so that true and unadulterated physical intimacy and fulfillment can take place..

For men, some of the erogenous zones are different and some are the same. When we think of them for the male, this is usually the list that comes to mind: the penis, the mouth and lips, the scrotum, the neck, and the ears. However, there are a couple of areas we tend to neglect on men that are also innately erogenous, and those areas are the nipples and the perineum.

What is a perineum? Well, it is the small area between the scrotum and the anus. It is a thin strip of skin that is acutely sensitive to touch. This area is the area of the male you will want to massage if they are having a hard time finding where to focus energy. Just like the clitoris on a female, it can be used to easily trigger a state of relaxation and help induce the idea of a calm and stress-free mind.

The nipples are a neglected area of the male that can be massaged, and should be massaged, during a tantric massage. While men's nipples are essentially by-products of evolution, they house the same nerve endings that women's nipples do. This means that, by stimulating them to peaks, you can help the blood circulation around the male's heart, which can lead to a stabilizing of the heart rate.

Just like with women, the ultimate goal of tantric massage for a man is to get him to clear his mind and open up his body to the realm of the universe beckoning for him. The muscles of his body will release, the chemicals and fluids flowing throughout his body will not be stopped by any blockages, his body will begin to heal and dispel harmful toxins it has been holding onto, and places that are not usually erogenous will become so. Areas on men such as the areas behind the ear, between the toes, and around the navel that are not usually sensitive will slowly become sensitive to the massaging touch, and that is how their partner (or masseur) will know the massage is finally working the way it should.

Now that you understand what an erogenous zone actually is and what it is used for in the context of tantric massage and what you need to look for as these zones continue to emerge and develop during the massage, it is time to talk about the different massage techniques that are useful when administering a tantric massage.

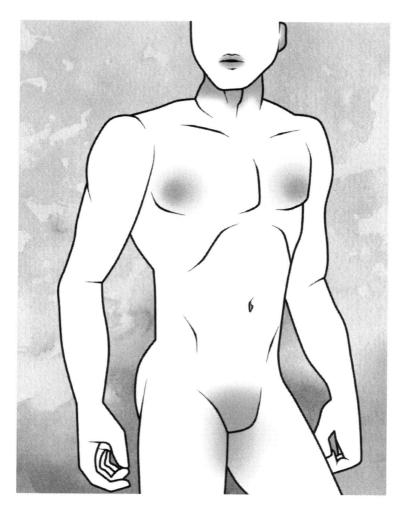

*The male erogenous zones, as highlighted in this illustration, are the penis, the mouth and lips, the scrotum, the neck, the ears, the nipples and perineum.*

# 8 SETTING THE SCENE

WHEN ENGAGING IN A TANTRA massage with your partner, you want to make sure the environment is as conducive to relaxing and opening up to the universe as possible. It can be difficult to relax and enjoy your massage if you have just rushed through the door after a stressful day from work, you can hear the honking of cars on the street, and you notice how you need to sweep the floor as you lay on your bed.

Making the time to lay the right scene for a sensual and erotic massage will help both you and your partner enjoy the experience more. There are a few things you can do to make sure you set the right "stage" or "scene" for tantric massage, and we'll get into those in this chapter.

The first thing you can do is make time for your tantric massage. Instead of trying to fit it in when you or your partner may be stressed or tired, plan at least a few days in advance so you can make sure to get in the right mindset before the massage takes place.

The next step of a tantric massage session is have an open mindset. You need to be open to exploring new parts of yourself, and experiencing new things. At first, it may be hard to relax and you may feel embarrassed or foolish. You can express these feelings to your partner and by doing so will feel a greater connection to yourself and him or her. It may sound or feel awkward, but opening yourself up to tantra can really be life-changing.

The next step is to make sure the environment is set up to promote the most relaxing environment. If you are going to use the bedroom, make it feel like it is not your regular bedroom, but a new haven of relaxation and sensuality. Light some candles, drape a tablecloth or blanket over unsightly piles or mess if they cannot be tidied quickly. Dim the lights or only use low lighting or lamps, put new sheets or a soft blanket on the bed. Put on soothing, soft music, and make sure the temperature of the room is not uncomfortable. Maybe take a bath before your tantra massage as well.

Before you begin the tantra massage, you and your partner can do some light stretching together to ease both of your bodies and loosen you up. You will be able to feel more intense pleasure if you are loose and un-tense to begin with. You can also meditate with your partner. If you are new to meditation, just set a timer and focus on taking slow, deep breaths for one minute. You can also meditate with your eyes open and look into each other's eyes, as this will connect you even more deeply. Have you ever noticed that people only hold each other's gaze for six seconds maximum? Any longer feels intrusive and intimate, and it may be so for friends or acquaintances, it will be a pleasurable experience to have with your trusted partner. It sounds simple, but just gazing into someone else's eyes is a deep experience, and it will set the mood for the tantra massage. Try to do at least 5 minutes, and go for 10 if you feel comfortable.

Before you begin, you may want to sit in the traditional Yab Yum tantric pose. In this pose, the male sits cross legged, and the female sits in his lap, facing him, with her legs wrapped around. You may continue to look into each other's eyes or perform breathing meditations.

These simple steps will get you ready for a tantric massage session with relaxation and closeness.

# 9 Tantric Massage Techniques

When it comes to tantric massage, there are many different variations from the basics. In this chapter, we will talk you through how to do these basic foundational massage strokes, and from there you can collaborate with your partner to find out what they enjoyed best, what helped them to relax the best, and alter them in ways that will ultimately suit your own purposes. First and foremost, however, it is important to understand that most massages start with the person on their stomach. Because the back harnesses almost one-third of the muscles in the entire body, it is imperative to spend a great deal of time on the neck, shoulders, and back of an individual. Then, when they are fully relaxed, they can turn over and you can continue the tantric massage from the temples all the way down to the toes.

The first motion begins simply with covering the recipient of the massage in warmed oil. This will help cut down on the friction between your hands and their skin. You can use scented oil to give an extra relaxing boost to someone who might be struggling to do so. Begin by pouring two tablespoons of oil into the palms of your hands and rub them together to warm them—and the oil—up. You do not want to shock the recipient with cold, but you do not want the oil to be hotter than body temperature. Remember, this is all about relaxation. Once the oil is warmed, use fluid motions to spread the oil onto the recipient's back, neck, buttocks, and the backs of their legs.

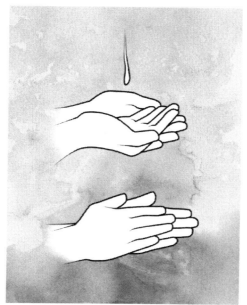

*Begin by pouring two tablespoons of oil into the palms of your hands and rub them together to warm them—and the oil—up*

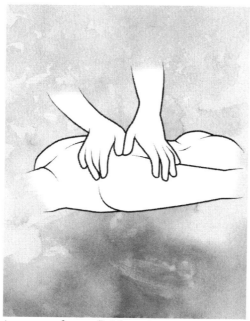

*Once the oil is warmed, use fluid motions to spread the oil onto the recipient's back, neck, buttocks, and the backs of their legs.*

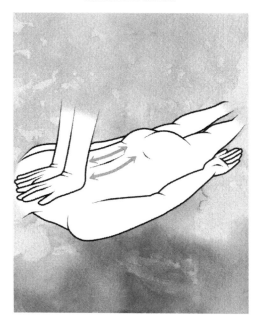

*"Hand Slide"*

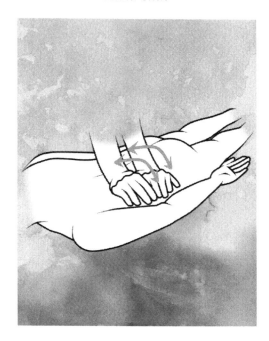

*"Pull-Up"*

Then it is time to use your first massage technique. It is called the "hand slide," and it is very simple: put your hands on the recipient parallel to one another with your fingers pointing up toward their head. Then, slowly apply pressure and slide your hands upwards. Once you reach the end of the muscle, slowly slide your hands back down the same path they came. If you want to do one fluid stroke to get them relaxed, place your hands in the crook of their lower back, slowly slide them up and around their shoulders, and then drag your hands all the way back down to their buttocks. This touches on most of the muscles in the back and will ease the recipient of the massage into a relaxed state of body and mind.

Now, it is time for the massage technique called the "pull-up." This is where you place your well-oiled hands on either side of the person's body, press down lightly, and then gently push them up toward the spine. The movements should be coming in almost perpendicular to the spine, and you should be using your body weight as a pressure gauge. You can either put one hand on either side and straddle the recipient when doing this, or you can stand at either side of them and use both hands at once on one side of the body.

Then, there is kneading. If you have ever seen someone knead bread dough or watched a cat settle down for a nap by kneading the surface with its paws, you are familiar with this movement. If you have never done this, the best place to start is with your partner's buttocks. Place your hands on their buttock cheeks and squeeze. Start with your fingers spread wide and close them together over the recipient's skin. This will help to prime muscles that get more action than others for the relaxation to come. Understand, kneading will take a bit more pressure to work, so be careful with where you use this type of motion. You wouldn't want to use this same pressing motion on something as sensitive as a woman's breasts!

Then, there is the feather stroke. This is where you take your fingertips and lightly run them up and down areas of the body for a certain amount of time. Areas like the neck, arms, and thighs can really benefit from something like this, especially if a deeper massage technique is necessary in order to get these areas of the body to relax. You can do long fluid lines or light circular motions, but the point is to "feather" your fingertips across their skin in a repetitive motion of your choosing.

*"Kneading"*

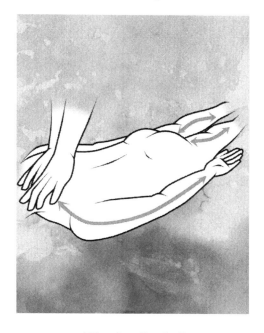

*"Feather Stroke"*

Then, there is the foot caress. This is specifically for the foot, so whenever you are ready to try this go ahead and stand at your partner's feet. At this point, you will probably need more oil, so don't hesitate to reach for it. The first motion in the foot caress is to do the hand slide technique all the way down the back of the thigh and calf. Then, back it up with a bit of kneading on the thigh and calf as well. Do one leg at a time when you are doing this and make sure the muscles are fully relaxed before you move onto the feet. If you don't, and your partner is ticklish, you will get kicked! (You may also ruin the mood of the massage).

Once you know your partner is good and relaxed, take one foot at a time and smother it in oil. Spread it around the ankle, the heel, and even between their toes! Once you are done covering it in the oily goodness, utilize the palm and the heel of your hand in order slide over the bottom of your partner's feet. Do a broad motion three or four times, and then go to turning your partner's ankle. Slowly rotate their foot clockwise and counterclockwise to relax their ankles, and then go back to the broad sliding of your palm over the bottom of their feet. Then, once you have done all of that, gently pull each toe away from the body. This will help stretch those little joints that take such a beating throughout the day, and you will be surprised the relief your partner will begin to feel!

Then, it is time to turn your partner over and allow them to experience those same massage techniques on their front. Remember, the front of the body cannot take as much as the back, so be careful where you knead and how much pressure you apply.

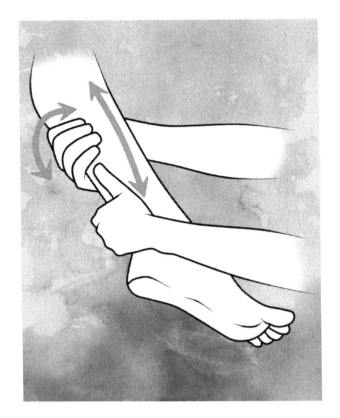

*"Foot Caress"*

# 10 TANTRIC BREATHING TECHNIQUES

ANOTHER THING TO TAKE INTO consideration when administering a tantric massage is walking your partner through several series of breathing techniques. There are three basic breathing techniques to help with relaxation and the centering of the mind when it comes to aligning the body's chakras with the universe, and they are all important to use as the relaxation and physical fulfillment of the massage deepens for the recipient.

The first, and most fundamental, is the deep breath. This is usually done during the long hand glide strokes, and the recipient of the massage should time their breaths with the strokes. Breathe deeply through the nose for four beats, and then release lightly through the mouth for four beats. This is the initial breathing sequence that helps to center the mind and rid it of all the cluttering thoughts that whiz through it throughout the day.

Once the recipient becomes relaxed and their mind is beginning to clear, the breathing technique they can start using is called the "puffing air." This is a breathing technique that should take place during times where the body is being kneaded, but should only happen if the recipient of the massage is on their back. This is when short puffs of air are exhaled sharply through the lips, and the stomach should contract with each puff of air. When air is brought back into the lungs, it should also come in through the lips, but the shoulders should not raise when the air is being brought in. It is a noisy breathing exercise, but it helps to promote the ridding of toxins from the body while the kneading massage technique is expelling them from the muscles.

The third breathing technique the masseuse should be talking the recipient through is called labor breaths, and it is similar to the breathing technique women are taught to use during labor. In this breathing technique, you will inhale two short puffs of air through your lips before exhaling one long breath through your nose. This is a breathing exercise that takes a great deal of mental capacity to do because it does not come naturally, so this should only be employed for individuals that come in to receive a tantric massage whose thoughts are either very clouded or who are incredibly tense. This helps to get them prepared to release themselves to the universe. It gives them something to control while much-needed oxygen floods their body, enabling them to eventually relax.

As a bonus, a fourth breathing technique, simply entitled "big breaths" can be used during tantric massage. This is where you take massive mouthfuls of air in slowly through your mouth before puckering your lips and releasing that same stash of air back through your lips. If someone is nervous about the massage, or if they begin experiencing anxieties during the massage, this breathing technique will help them to get much-needed oxygen into their bodies. It is the quickest way to intake air, and then the puckering of the lips helps to steady the breath coming out. If you release the breath too quickly, you will become light-headed, just like if you were to hyperventilate. This breathing technique is also a bit louder than normal breathing, so it will automatically signal to the masseuse that something is not right, and it will prompt conversation, or even a pause in the massage.

This breathing technique is not necessarily talked through, but talked about. The goal is to talk about the underlying cause of what prompted this type of breathing technique in the first place, and it helps to guide both the masseuse and the recipient of the massage past the bump that has occurred.

# 11 Is Tantric Massage Right For You?

Even with all the fluid motions and breathing techniques you have learned in the last chapters, how do you know if a tantric massage is right for you? Maybe you're not interested in opening your body to the universe or getting to know yourself any better than you already do.

What if you are looking for a way to relieve stress? Or take care of some chronic pain? Or what if you are looking to add something to your medication regimen to help you deal with your chronic depression or anxiety?

The great part about tantric massage is that it comes with all the medical benefits of a regular massage, with a few extra bonuses thrown into the mix.

There are many reasons why a tantric massage is right for an individual. If you are someone who has a loving and devoted partner and the two of you either want to become closer to one another, or the both of you want to become closer with the universe, then a tantric massage is most certainly right for you.

But what if you do not have a partner? Or you do not trust the partner you do have? Maybe you have some trauma want to overcome or some pain to work through. Maybe you are just interested in the idea of tantric massage.

This is the beauty of a tantric massage: because its true nature is not sexually-focused, it opens the door for treating a host of other issues. As mentioned earlier, it helps those who have experienced some type of trauma they have been looking to overcome work through their experience. The trauma could sexual, physical, psychological, or emotional, but in any case, because tantric massage aids the body in relaxing and aligning itself with the universe, this fulfillment without vulnerability can be an incredibly releasing experience for someone harboring these types of anxieties.

A tantric massage can also help with blood circulation issues, as well as help relieve massive amounts of stress from the body. The relaxation techniques enable the muscles to relax themselves instead of staying contracted because of the stress hormone cortisol, and this allows the body to let go of harmful chemicals and substances it has been holding onto because of the constant state of contraction the body has been in. This then allows the body to promote its own healing mechanisms, which can jumpstart the body's process of reviving its energy stores.

A tantric massage is also beneficial for those who are battling chronic aches and pains. Joint pain, inflammatory issues, and other chronic illnesses can be addressed with a tantric massage. Because this type of massage comes from the idea of attending to every single crevice of the body, those who experience joint pain will have every joint they experience pain with massaged thoroughly. This can help alleviate the fluids that build up around these joints, releasing this excess fluid back into the body to be discarded as waste. This, in turn, allows for inflammation in the body to dwindle, which can help the pain levels of people with that type of pain.

It can even help with cravings. From nicotine and substance cravings to craving sweets while on a diet, because of the centering force of a tantric massage, it helps to ward off those cravings. Because of the self-awareness and the physical fulfillment a tantric massage brings and enables, it helps the individual to find what it is they are missing rather than trying to fill the emptiness with something they do not actually need.

If you fall under any of these categories, or are simply looking for a way to relax, then a tantric massage is right for you. It can be something as distinct as getting rid of a bad habit or craving, or something as broad as helping you to manage your social anxiety. Whatever the case might be, if it is trauma-based, anxiety-based, panic-based, or stress-based, a tantric massage can help you cope.

## 12  EXPLORING TANTRIC SEX

WHEN A TANTRIC MASSAGE IS done with a loving, trusted partner, it may lead naturally into penetration or more sexual arousal. Moving from a tantric massage to a massage that addresses the sex organs that lead to orgasm should be fluid and feel natural, not forced.

Do not rush into what is thought in traditional Western culture as sex right away, but allow it to develop naturally for both partners. The masseuse should be paying attention to the cues and responses of the person's body they are massaging, and react accordingly with their touch.

Remember, the goal of tantric massage and even tantric sex is not to orgasm, but to feel closer to each other, to your spirituality, and to the universe. Go slow as you move into sexual penetration or touching, and connect deeply with the physical feelings you experience. Feel your heartbeat, focus on your breath, and bring together your genitals in a soft, loving way. Thrust slowly and intentionally together, to keep the experience one of spiritual tantra, and not just physical desire. You may also engage in tantric kissing, which focuses deeply on the breath and uniting two people as one. Feel as though you are breathing together and sharing breath, and continue to remain aware of your bodies.

Both partners may orgasm, or neither may. In the end, the experience you have is more powerful than a "goal" of tantra massage.

What makes a good tantra massage position? Whatever feels right and keeps things spiritual, deeply moving and connected to your body can be a tantra position. But the most well-known tantra massage position derives from the lotus position, and a common position used in meditation practices. It is called the Yab Yum pose and is the traditional tantric sex position. If you are familiar with crossing your legs and sitting on the floor, you understand what this position looks like. This position allows for both partner's sexual energy stores to open to the world and each other, and be fully embraced. In this position, the man sits cross-legged and the woman sits in his lap, facing him, with her legs wrapped around his torso.

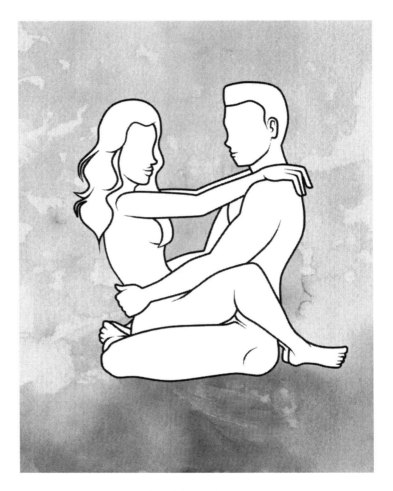

*"Yab Yum"*

Another position that is good for tantric sex is the colloquially-called "spooning" position. Here we will call it the cradling position. This allows both partners to be exceptionally close to each other physically, and for thrusting to be slow. This is a good way to transition from general massage techniques to penetration or more genital touching, and a good way to stay connected to the overall spiritual experience.

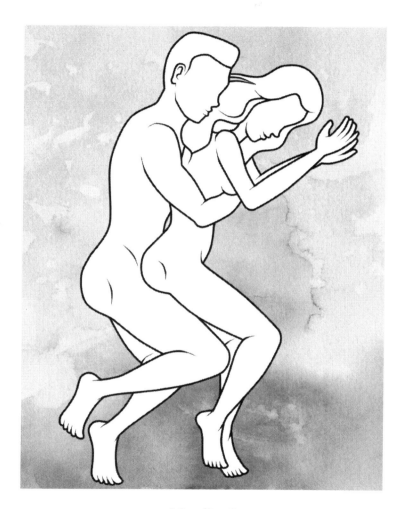

*"Cradling"*

Overall, any position that makes you feel a part of tantra massage is good to use, and remember to take it slow and not rush things or get too wrapped up in traditional Western sex constraints or the need to orgasm.

Here are a few more positions you can use to heighten bodily awareness, contact between partners, and intimacy and spirituality:

*"Lotus"*

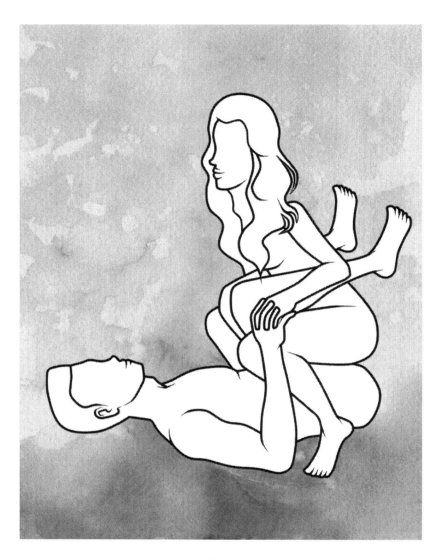

*"Fox"*

*"Waterfall"*

# 13 CONCLUSION

WHEN IT COMES TO GIVING a tantric massage, it is all about two things: the movements you use and the breathing techniques you coach your partner through. Both of these things combine to produce the most relaxing and mind-clearing experience for the person you are massaging and aid in your connection to them. While the highest percentage of benefits that come from a tantric massage come from giving or receiving a tantric massage from someone you love and trust, this does not mean a professional cannot help you benefit from one. A tantric massage is about opening up your mind, body, soul, and spirit to the universal energies that surround us on a daily basis. It is about fulfilling all basic aspects of human drive and survival without feeling guilt, and it is about finding that perfect balance between unfulfilled and gluttonous.

We will die if we do not drink water, but drinking too much water can cause water poisoning and cell death. Not eating enough means starvation, but eating too much leads to bad health and obesity. Likewise, not fulfilling the physical intimacy aspect of life leads to mental and emotional stressors we cannot cope with, while fulfilling it too much causes a great disconnect between the body's emotional stores and the energies of the universe. The key is balance.

When you are giving a tantric massage, there is one thing you must be aware of, and that is the reason you are giving the massage in the first place. If you are giving it solely for someone to chase a temporary high, or an orgasm, then the massage will only leave you both unfulfilled. However, if you are giving the massage to someone who is attempting to overcome trauma, become closer to you, or to really give their bodies over to the expansive universe that has breathed life into our beings, then that is very important to understand. How the recipient of the massage is utilizing the massage will help you to better connect with the person you are massaging. That knowledge is imperative because it will allow you a context through which to interpret the recipient's body language and sounds throughout the process.

If you are receiving a massage, then understand this: knowing the purpose for receiving one is key. It helps the masseur to guide you through the expansive massage, and the more knowledge the masseuse has, the better it will work for you. Being on the receiving end of the massage also allows you a chance to become more self-aware. When someone is giving a massage, they are wholly focused on the person in front of them. This means their own connection to the universe and their own self-awareness gets put on hold for you. Take this time to delve deep into the pits of your mind and learn more about yourself.

Maybe there is a goal you have in your life that you have cast aside for the time being. Maybe there is a trial you are experiencing in your life that you don't know how to navigate. Maybe there is a great love, a great heartache, or a great medical or financial pain you have no idea how to battle.

Whatever the case might be, opening yourself up to the universe around you will not just fill you with physical energies to help you get through your days, it will also help center and guide your mind so you can have the clear head to make the decisions you need to make. Those decisions should not be made while you are receiving the massage, as those decisions might cause unnecessary stress to creep into your body, but clearing your mind and opening your soul will help you ease that process later.

It works a little like the great coin trick: if you have a decision you need to make, but have no idea where you stand, then find a coin and put it in your hand. In your mind, you designate heads as one decision and tails as the other. Then, you throw the coin up into the air and let it plummet to the ground. The idea is that when you base the outcome of your decision on something you have no way of controlling, your true feelings will emerge. You will find yourself rooting for one side to show up over the other.

During a tantric massage, when you clear your mind and open your soul to the influence of the universe, you will find that the universe pushes you in a specific direction. Once you give your control over to your base chakras, the universe will re-energize you via this tantric massage, and the decision you have been struggling to make will almost suddenly be decided.

That is the incredible benefit of the tantric massage. It isn't just about the idea of aligning oneself with the universe. It is about self-awareness, physical and emotional intimacy, and establishing a connection with the world around you instead of merely attempting to navigate around it.

Welcome to the world of tantric massage.

Hopefully now, it is no longer misunderstood.

# Your Feedback is Important to Me

Dear Reader,

Thank you for taking the time to read this book. I hope you got a lot out of it and learned something you can apply to your own life.

If you have any feedback, positive or negative, I'd love to hear from you. I personally read all the reviews on my Amazon page, and hope you'll take a minute to tell me (and other readers) what you think.

Type this URL into your browser to go straight to the review page for this book: bitly.com/tantricreview

Thank you!

—Rozella Hart

# FURTHER READING

## More sensual titles from Walnut Publishing:

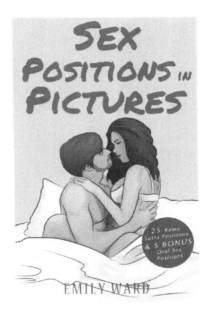

"25 Sex Positions in Pictures,"
an illustrated sex guide by Emily Ward

Available in Ebook ($2.99), Paperback ($5.99) & Audiobook ($2.99) on
Amazon at:

bitly.com/sexposillus

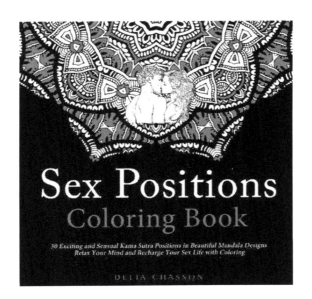

"Sex Positions Coloring Book,"

a saucy adult coloring book for pleasure and creativity

Available in paperback ($5.99) on Amazon at:

bitly.com/sexycoloring

## More titles from author Rozella Hart:

"Dream Journal,"

a guide to revealing the true meaning behind your subconscious

Available in Ebook ($0.99) and Paperback ($5.99) on Amazon at:

bitly.com/dreampages

"Empath,"

a guide to relationships boundaries and thriving in a chaotic world

Available in Ebook ($0.99) and Paperback ($4.49) on Amazon at:

bitly.com/empathbook

21674235R00035

Printed in Poland
by Amazon Fulfillment
Poland Sp. z o.o., Wrocław